EPM

When you feel lost,
spend time with Nature.

You will find yourself
and therefore, your path.

Eric Patrick Marr
1890 Star Shoot Pkwy Ste. 170-144
Lexington, KY 40509
www.EricPatrickMarr.com

Ordering information is at www.EricPatrickMarr.com

Print ISBN: 978-1-66785-908-8
eBook ISBN: 978-1-66785-910-1

Printed in the United States of America on SFI Certified paper.

First Edition

Natural Law

It doesn't take an expert. It just takes a look.

Eric Patrick Marr

EricPatrickMarr.com

Acknowledgments

Our Oceans

Lia Davidson, Editor

Seth Godin's *Writing in Community* workshop

Thomas Paine, Author of *Common Sense*

Preface

On one hand, writing this book was daunting because many today take pride in showing off how offended they can appear.

On the other hand, this book writes itself and doesn't need my help. The data is in front of us whether we acknowledge it or not.

The best conversations are the hard ones, the ones we hold back for entirely too long.

Eric P. Marr

> *"If one way be better than another,*
> *that you may be sure is nature's way."*

Aristotle

Eric P. Mann

The Gist

Nature – and America - on paper
are intended to be synonymous.

But we've strayed from both.

America isn't meant to center around hysteria, nor any
person. Not a President, Congressman, or Governor.
America's premise is the self-evident recognition that *you*
own your life; that *you* were endowed by Mother Nature
with the inherent right *to make your own choices.*

Now, it's up to you what you do.

Eric P. Marr

Contents

Chapter 1

Natural Law

*"Never, no never, did Nature say one thing,
and wisdom another."*

Edmund Burke

Eric P. Marr

/ nat • u • ral /

existing in or caused by nature;

not made or caused by humankind

/ law /

a rule defining correct procedure

Eric P. Marr

Imagine if only you and your five best friends were living on Earth.[i]

You might be the happiest you could ever be.

Peace. Harmony. Ease.

Life with few obstacles and next to no stress.

You probably wouldn't have any formal societal structure, nor a government as we know it.

_____

Then something happens...

When we start trying to exert authority over others, ***trouble ensues.*** Conflicts. Unrest.

Eric P. Marr

There is only one solution to this: to keep aligned with Nature. To remember how we got here in the first place. To remember that *Nature* created us – and each equally and sovereignly.

You didn't create yourself. I didn't create myself.

Because Nature created us, she makes the rules. She's the one who gives us our rights - they don't come from other people. ***Therefore, no one can take them away.***

Our decisions determine our outcomes.

Chapter 2

America's Premise

is Natural Law

Something might be normal, but is it Natural?

Eric

Don't take my word for it.

Get it straight from the horses' mouths.

Eric P. Marr

* * *

"When in the course of human events, it becomes necessary for a people to dissolve the political bands which have connected them with another, and to assume among the powers of the Earth the separate and equal station **to which the Laws of Nature and of Nature's God entitle them,** a decent respect to the opinions of mankind requires that they should declare the causes which impel them to the separation."

The very first sentence of our
American Declaration of Independence

* * *

Eric P. Marr

* * *

"Mankind possesses rights antecedent

to all earthly government.

Rights that cannot be repealed or restrained

by human laws.

Rights derived from the great Legislator of the universe."

John Adams, 2nd U.S. President

* * *

"Freedom is not a gift bestowed upon us by other men, but

a right that belongs to us by the laws of God *and nature.*"

Benjamin Franklin, 1807

* * *

* * *

"The fundamental source of all your errors, sophisms, and false reasoning *is a total ignorance of the natural rights of mankind.* Were you once to become acquainted with these, you could never entertain a thought that all men are not, by nature, entitled to a parity of privileges.

You would be convinced that natural liberty is a gift of the beneficent Creator, to the whole human race; and that civil liberty is founded in that; and cannot be wrested from any people, without the most manifest violation of justice."

Alexander Hamilton, 1775

* * *

Eric P. Marr

America's foundation, however, is eroding.

We have strayed from Nature.

Making us vulnerable to enemies,

both domestic and abroad.

Chapter 3

The Problem

"He who dares not offend cannot be honest."

Thomas Paine

Let's start at the top. Ultimately, our physical health determines everything.

1. America is the #1 most obese country in the developed world today.[ii]

2. 2/3 of us are overweight or outright obese.[iii]

3. 3/4 of us don't exercise enough.[iv]

4. 90% of us don't eat fruits and vegetables.[v]

5. *More of us smoke cigarettes* than eat fruits and vegetables.[vi, vii]

We eat terribly and we don't exercise. There's no other way to say it. And our habits greatly degrade our *naturally* bestowed immune systems, leaving our bodies vulnerable to a myriad of diseases.

Case in point: Guess what the #1 leading cause of severe sickness or death during the COVID-19 pandemic among non-senior citizens was.

Obesity. [viii, ix, x, xi, xii, xiii, xiv]

* * *

73% of deceased COVID-19 patients had obesity or were overweight

U.S. Center for Disease Control [xv]

* * *

This is our *true* American public health emergency – and it's been accumulating for decades. [xvi]

And our individual health doesn't just affect us as individuals anymore – today it spills over onto everyone else.

When 2/3 - 3/4 of us are obese or overweight, and a virus comes along like COVID-19, *everyone* is commanded to shut down their businesses, their children's schools, their churches... their lives.

It wouldn't be such an emergency if we took better care of our bodies to start with, keeping our natural immune systems as strong as they can be.

The term "hospital capacity" was all the rage, *but who most often lands in the hospital?* Us, when we don't take care of ourselves to begin with.

Eric P. Marr

In addition, our lifestyle habits render us physically weaker to defend ourselves against foreign enemies. Think: Vladimir Putin, North Korea, and terrorists.

Nearly 1 in 3 young American adults are too obese to even serve in our U.S. Military.[xvii]

It is unrealistic to expect positive outcomes when 62-75% of society is weakened and prone to sickness or death.

It's unnatural.

The Problem, Part II:

Our Politicians

Wouldn't you think that our society's leaders, who are supposed to be "on our team," would do things to help our country be its best?

Yeah, you'd think.

But our loudest social voices actually exacerbate the problem. They literally make matters worse.

Eric P. Marr

The Problem, Part II-A:

Politicians Make Terrible Scientists

"Science," per many of today's politicians

Eric P. Marr

How many politicians have you seen hold press conferences encouraging us to eat better and get some exercise? Compared to, say, mandating injections into our bodies and masks on our faces? Mandating governmental shutdowns of schools, businesses, churches - and life?

From 2020 into 2022, all we read about were the grave dangers of Coronavirus. We never heard a peep - and still don't, today - about how our own choices *create most of these problems to start with.*

Personal responsibility - *natural law* - gets completely dismissed and ignored by our politicians.

As does actual science.

Why is natural immunity to COVID-19 from prior infection almost never discussed by our politicians, when data repeatedly shows it to be at least as effective as the mRNA vaccines?[xviii]

Why not stand in front of all those cameras and share the CDC's data that only 10-12% of us eat fruits and vegetables which strengthen our bodies with vital nutrients to fend off diseases?

Why do our convenience stores and street corners practically only sell junk food or fast food – yet that's never the focus of any politician's press conference?

If our politicians are all about public health and science, why do we live in a country where you can drive past nearly any hospital and literally see patients, nurses, and doctors standing outside *smoking cigarettes?*

Why aren't our weakened natural immune systems

Eric P. Marr

– because 90% of us are malnourished and 70% of us overweight or obese – ever discussed as the actual underlying problem?

How come they don't publicly encourage us to get more exercise, to strengthen our bodies that way?

All *the actual* science clearly points to all these things being our true, fundamental problems.

And isn't it their sworn duty to protect America from foreign enemies? Then why don't they discuss the deterioration of our youth's health and fitness, which is imperative to our military readiness? Why have they allowed 31% of our young adults to be so unhealthy they aren't even qualified to serve?[xix]

They pick and choose which "science" they want to peddle.

Why?

Because they want votes.

Our political and governmental systems are actually working against us. Instead of creating pathways for us to live healthier and stronger, they are only protecting politicians' career ambitions.

The Problem, Part II-B:

Our Politicians Dismiss Natural Law

"All the great laws of society

are laws of Nature."

Thomas Paine, *Rights of Man*, 1791

Not only do our politicians pick and choose which "science" they peddle, they also bypass the hard job of sparking conversations about our legitimate health needs. What's more, *they also compound the problem* by breaking Natural Law with their complete ignorance - *or dismissal of* - our Natural equality.

Case in point: the one-man executive order. A single man or woman deciding what millions of equal citizens can or cannot do. *Nothing could be less natural or less American.*

The Coronavirus pandemic saw the abuse of the executive mandate across America, with emergency orders fabricated beyond all normal, historical and common sense uses. Meanwhile, unnatural, illegitimate authority directly degrades mankind's mental, emotional and intellectual state.

Governors and political figures addressing citizens as if they are our saviors and we are their subjects morally obliged to obey. American citizens being categorized *by who is essential and who isn't.*

Some politicians even labeled citizens "unpatriotic" if you disobeyed their mandates, *when America's entire premise*

Eric P. Marr

is that We the People decide our rules.

It's written right there in our Declaration: "Government derives its just powers (only) *from the consent of the governed.*"

Executive mandates like we saw during COVID-19 are a complete violation of our American Constitution's chief cornerstone. In America, we don't have rules decided for us by a King, a Governor, or a President. *In America, we decide our own rules,* specifically through our multiple representatives in our Houses and Senates, our *second* branches of our three.

Eric P. Marr

Natural Law

Government's constitutional – *and much more natural-* role is to share accurate information so that *we may make good decisions for ourselves.*

We were created by Nature; government *was not.*

Therefore, government has no natural rights. Therefore, *we are sovereign over it.*

Government is at our discretion; it is entirely a man-made entity.

Eric P. Marr

* * *

Educate vs. Mandate

"I know no safe depositary of the ultimate powers
of society but the people themselves,
and if we think them not enlightened enough to exercise
their control with a wholesome discretion, the remedy is
not to take it from them, but to inform their discretion by
education.

This is the true corrective of abuses
of constitutional power."

Thomas Jefferson

* * *

Author's Note:

Without question, some of our most famous American framers were unable - or unwilling - to apply the premises of sovereignty, equality, freedom and Natural Rights to the real world, at the unspeakable expense of innumerable lives.

I am not suggesting our founders were at all, not the least bit, above reproach.

*My point is that America **is supposed to be** grounded in Natural Law, where every single Person is sovereign and equal in Nature's eyes.*

Self-evidently.

A concept we still wrestle with today.

Eric P. Marr

The Problem, Part III:

Our Media Peddles Junk Food

Never forget: Media is a business and businesses *rely on customers.* More specifically, most media today is an *entertainment* business. Producers create content they know we'll buy so they can compete in the vast, modern marketplace.

It reminds me of my grandma. She always had candy waiting for us whenever we visited. Notice: *media outlets and sweet grandmas never set asparagus or broccoli out for us. Businesswise, they want to win us over - and that's easier accomplished with junk food.*

Fear, hype, hysteria and drama win clicks, eyeballs and viewers. Think about it: No one watches the weather super religiously *unless there's a storm brewing.* Then, we're all glued to the set!

Meanwhile, social media's *entire existence* is built upon keeping us addicted to their constant sugar.

No wonder our collective intellectualism and our public discourse have eroded so dramatically in the last decade or so. All we're consuming is junk food. *Today's media literally encourages feuding and discord. Today's media sells stress.*

Drama garners attention. And more attention means more advertising revenue.

Eric P. Marr

The Problem, Part IV

Our Mental Health

"Man's heart away from Nature becomes hard."

Chief Standing Bear

Natural Law

Why does it matter what our politicians say and do? What media headlines feed us? Because a great many of our own thoughts and choices are directly influenced by what we see and hear around us.

Our environments tremendously affect our minds and bodies. Consider: a stressful workplace, a stressful relationship, a stressful *anyplace.*

Which is why - if we really want society to advance and improve – we must have community cultures that empower each of us to think our best and be our best. (Think: the opposite of how things have been lately.)

Our political leaders, media channels and social voices play an enormous role in how we live and function – or don't.

Eric P. Marr

If they're spreading fear and stress, what do you think the consequences will be? Now imagine if they'd instead instill hope, optimism and confidence.

Our own government is especially impactful on our mental state *because it has the unique ability to punish, to criminalize.* When governments begin treating its own citizens as inferior, as if Mother Nature endowed only them with rights but not us, it says one thing to the mind: **"You are small."**

This condescension kills you – and society - from the inside out.

Neither we nor society at large can progress when we are commanded to still our voices, to not think for ourselves, to not take part in the natural order of life.

And because it's so unnatural for one Person to set himself above another, it throws humanity into complete chaos.

* * *

"It is the pride of kings which throws mankind into confusion."

Thomas Paine, *Common Sense*, 1776

* * *

Think about when we've had the most social unrest in our country. It's always been when inequality has reared its head, when manipulative people have tried to exert authority over other equal Persons.

Eric P. Marr

Chapter 4

Our Solution

Society is at its best when individuals are enabled to be their best.

Eric

No one person has everyone else's answers. (That's the point of Chapter Three!) *You* are best equipped to know the best for *your* life.

But aligning with Nature is our common prerequisite.

How we take care of our bodies. How we tend to our minds. How we design our workdays and workplaces. How we build our society. There are many solutions available to us, but if our choices do not work with Nature, we're dead in the water.

The point of this book is that ***these conversations need to be had.*** We can't keep ignoring what's all around us, pretending that Nature doesn't matter. It ***does*** matter. To the billionth, trillionth degree.

We are not free as individuals, or as a society, when we disregard Nature's ways. Enemies of some sort rule over us when we remain misaligned with her.

Eric P. Marr

* * *

"If a nation expects to be ignorant and free – in a state of civilization – it expects what never was and never will be."

Thomas Jefferson

* * *

For my part, who knows what the road ahead holds. With the publication of this book, I do know I'm going to continue these public conversations with much more in-depth podcasts and blogs about all these topics.

I'm also launching a brand new business I believe will help. "15" is based on my own work and life experiences that actively pursuing goals is extraordinarily healthy. We just also need encouraging surroundings to help us consistently go after these larger aspirations.

"15" combines these into one. I've seen it work time and time again, just naturally.

I look forward to hearing and seeing *your* solutions.

* * *

"Like music and art, love of nature is a common language that can transcend political or social boundaries."

U.S. President Jimmy Carter

* * *

Eric P. Marr

ADDITIONAL

RESOURCES

Eric P. Marr

Our Health, Physical & Mental

40% of Americans are obese; another 32% are overweight.

- CDC.gov

Estimate: Half of US adults will be obese by 2030

- ABC News

Obesity may reduce COVID-19 vaccine efficacy

- News-Medical.net

Obesity is the second most preventable cause of death after smoking.

- San Diego Tribune

Economic Impact of Obesity

The estimated annual medical cost of obesity in the United States was $147 billion in 2008. (= $196B in 2022)
Medical costs for people who had obesity was $1,429 higher than medical costs for people with healthy weight (2008)

- CDC.gov

Eric P. Marr

Malnourishment in the U.S.

Vitamins are Important to our Immune Systems

- CDC.gov

Hypocrisy & Politicians: COVID-19 vs. Tobacco Education

Politicians have been all about "following CDC guidelines" during the COVID-19 pandemic.

But why don't politicians also invest CDC-recommended levels into tobacco education to save lives?

States have billions of dollars from the taxes they put on tobacco products and money from lawsuits against cigarette companies that they can use to prevent smoking and help smokers quit. Right now, though, the states only use a very small amount of that money to prevent and control tobacco use.

In fiscal year 2020, states will collect $27.2 billion from tobacco taxes and settlements in court but will only spend $740 million in the same year. That's only 2.7% of it spent on programs that can stop young people from becoming smokers and help current smokers quit. Right now, not a single state out of 50 funds these programs at CDC's "recommended" level. Only three states (Alaska, California, and Maine) give even 70% of the full recommended amount. Twenty-eight states and the District of Columbia spend less than 20% of what the CDC recommends. One state, Connecticut, gives no state funds for prevention and quit-smoking programs.

Spending 12% (about $3.3 billion) of the $27.2 billion would fund every state's tobacco control program at CDC-recommended levels.

- CDC.gov

The Tobacco Industry spent $8.2B on marketing in 2019.

- CDC.gov

Total economic cost of smoking is more than $300 billion a year, including $170 billion in direct medical care for adults, $156 billion in lost productivity due to premature death and exposure to secondhand smoke.

- National Library of Medicine

We spend 8 Hours Every Single Day on our Phones or Watching Television

Eric P. Marr

According to Nielsen's latest Total Audience Report, Americans adults spend over four hours a day watching TV, still beating the three hours and 45 minutes they interact with their smartphone on an average day by roughly half an hour.

- Statista.com

Americans spend $56 billion on sporting events. Half of that on books.

- CNBC.com

Global data, re: COVID-19 and obesity:

The World Obesity Federation research discovered 2.2 million of 2.5 million reported COVID-19 deaths worldwide, 88%, were in countries with high obesity rates.

- San Diego Tribune

Japan's Dietary Habits vs. America's

On average, Japanese people consume significantly less trans fat and 25 percent fewer calories than Americans. Japan's adult obesity is 4.3%. Japanese men have less than one-third of the coronary disease as U.S. men, partially from consuming ample fish high in Omega-3. Japanese male smokers are nearly seven

times less likely to develop lung cancer as U.S. male smokers. Japanese women are four to five times less likely to develop breast cancer as U.S. women. Japanese men have the world's lowest prostate cancer rate attributed to diet.
- San Diego Tribune

The COVID-19 death rate is ten times higher in countries where 50%+ of the population is overweight.
- British Medical Journal

The U.S. Declaration of Independence

When in the course of human events, it becomes necessary for one people to dissolve the political bands which have connected them with another, and to assume among the powers of the earth, the separate and equal station to which the Laws of Nature and of Nature's God entitle them, a decent respect to the opinions of mankind requires that they should declare the causes which impel them to the separation.

We hold these truths to be self-evident, that all men are created equal, that they are endowed by their Creator with certain unalienable Rights, that among these are Life, Liberty and the pursuit of Happiness. That to secure these rights, Governments are instituted among Men, deriving their just powers from the consent of the governed,

That whenever any Form of Government becomes destructive of these ends, it is the Right of the People to alter or to abolish it, and to institute new Government, laying its foundation on such principles and organizing its powers in such form, as to them shall seem most likely to effect their Safety and Happiness.

- National Archives

REFERENCES

---

[i] *Common Sense*, by Thomas Paine, 1776

[ii] **The U.S. is the most obese nation in the developed world.**

- MarketWatch.com

[iii] The United States is home to the highest number of overweight and obese people in the world.

In the U.S., 70.9% of men and 61.9% of women are overweight or obese, compared to 38% of men and 36.9% of women worldwide.

American Youth: 28.8% of boys and 29.7% of girls are overweight or obese in the U.S., compared to 14.2% of boys and 14.7% of girls worldwide.

- EverydayHealth.com

[iv] **76% of Americans Don't Get Enough Exercise**

As of 2017, only about 24% of Americans met the federal physical activity guidelines.

- Time.com

---

[v] **Americans don't eat enough fruits and vegetables.**
In 2015 and 2019, only about one in ten adults met recommendations for fruit and vegetable intake.

Eating a diet rich in fruits and vegetables can help protect against a number of serious and costly chronic diseases, including heart disease, type 2 diabetes, some cancers, and obesity.

- CDC.gov

[vi] The percentage of U.S. adults meeting fruit and vegetable intake recommendations is low. In 2019, 12.3% and 10.0% of surveyed adults met fruit and vegetable intake recommendations, respectively.

A dietary including sufficient fruits and vegetables can help protect against some chronic conditions that are among the leading causes of mortality in the United States; some of tare also associated with more severe illness from COVID-19.

- CDC.gov

[vii] **12.5% of American adults smoke cigarettes.**

– CDC.gov

[viii] The risk of severe COVID-19 illness increases sharply with elevated BMI. Overweight, obesity or severe obesity can make you more likely to get severely ill from COVID-19.

- CDC.gov

[ix] CDC: Adults with excess weight were at even greater risk during the COVID-19 pandemic:

- Obesity increases the risk of severe illness from COVID-19. People who are overweight may also be at increased risk.
- Obesity may triple the risk of hospitalization due to a COVID-19 infection.
- Obesity is linked to impaired immune function.
- Obesity decreases lung capacity and reserve and can make ventilation more difficult.
- A study of COVID-19 cases suggests that risks of hospitalization, intensive care unit admission, invasive mechanical ventilation, and death are higher with increasing BMI.
- The increased risk for hospitalization or death was particularly pronounced in those under age 65.

- CDC.gov

[x] Obesity emerged as a strong and independent risk factor for severe infection and death due to COVID-19.

- Obesity Action Coalition

[xi] People with obesity who contracted SARS-CoV-2 were 113% more likely than people of healthy weight to land in the hospital, 74% more likely to be admitted to an ICU, and 48% more likely to die.

- Science.org

[xii] Obesity was independently and strongly associated with hospitalization, need for oxygen therapy, higher viral load, and an altered immune response.

- US Military Health System (MHS)

[xiii] The CDC: 73% of deceased COVID-19 patients had obesity or were overweight.

- San Diego Tribune

[xiv] Among adults, 50.8% had obesity and 28.3% were overweight who received a COVID-19 diagnosis during an emergency

Eric P. Marr

department (ED) or inpatient visit at 238 U.S. hospitals during March–December 2020,

- CDC.gov

[xv] The CDC: 73% of deceased COVID-19 patients had obesity or were overweight.

- San Diego Tribune

[xvi] Obesity Prevalence in America: 42.4% in 2017-18

From 1999-2000 through 2017-18, obesity prevalence increased from 30.5% to 42.4%. During the same time, the prevalence of severe obesity increased from 4.7% to 9.2%.

- CDC.gov

[xvii] **Obesity's impact on our U.S. Military**

31% of young Americans are too obese to serve.

- StrongNation.org

[xviii] **Natural Immunity Against COVID-19 from Prior Infection**

Prior COVID-19 was associated with protection of 85% against any recurrent COVID-19, 88% against hospitalization for COVID-19, and 83% against COVID-19 not requiring

Eric P. Marr

hospitalization. Protection remained stable over the study period with no attenuation up to 9 months from initial infection.

Among 121,615 patients with more than 10 million days of follow-up, unvaccinated individuals with prior symptomatic COVID-19 had 85% lower risk of acquiring COVID-19 than unvaccinated individuals without prior COVID-19. Prior studies investigating protection against SARS-CoV-2 reinfection found similar results, with protection associated with natural immunity ranging from 80.5% to 100%.[2] This level of protection is similar to that reported for mRNA vaccines.

The findings that patients with prior COVID-19 had 88% protection against hospitalization for COVID-19 and 83% protection against COVID-19 not requiring hospitalization suggest that natural immunity was associated with similar protection against mild and severe disease. mRNA vaccines are associated with similar prolonged protection from severe COVID-19, although vaccine-associated protection from mild COVID-19 has been shown to wane at 6 months.

- Journal of the American Medical Association Network

[xix] Obesity's Impact on our U.S. Military (cont.)

"A study in 2018 found 31 percent of Americans ages 17-24 would not qualify for military service due to obesity. The military spends $1.5 billion annually to treat obesity-related health conditions, including replacement of unfit troops. The CDC reports retired military officials disclosed insurmountable obstacles recruiting adequate soldiers over the last 10 years, stressing the health decline of today's youth as cause, also warning unless our nation achieves significant improvements in physical activity and nutrition, our military readiness will become endangered, and thus our national security."

- San Diego Tribune